Harry Potter Beverage and Dessert Recipes

Unofficial Harry Potter Cookbook with Easy Recipes

By

Martha Stephenson

Copyright 2017 Martha Stephenson

License Notes

No part of this Book can be reproduced in any form or by any means including print, electronic, scanning or photocopying unless prior permission is granted by the author.

All ideas, suggestions and guidelines mentioned here are written for informative purposes. While the author has taken every possible step to ensure accuracy, all readers are advised to follow information at their own risk. The author cannot be held responsible for personal and/or commercial damages in case of misinterpreting and misunderstanding any part of this Book

Table of Contents

Introduction 5

    Butterbeer 7

    Pumpkin Juice 9

    Golden Snitch Cake Pops 11

    Butterbeer Hot Chocolate 13

    Knickerbocker Glory 15

    Bertie Bott's Jelly Beans 17

    Unicorn Blood Cocktail 19

    Polyjuice Potion 21

    Goblet of Fire 23

    The Albus Dumbledore 25

    Firewhiskey 27

    Pureblood 29

    The Phoenix Feather 31

    Liquid Luck 33

    Amortentia – The Love Potion 35

    Witches Brew 37

    The Severus Snape 39

Polyjuice Potion Jelly Shots 41

Voldemort Cocktail 43

Pumkintini 45

Butterbeer Jelly Shots 47

Chocolate Frog Jelly Shots 49

Confunda Chambardo 51

Avada Tequila 53

Butterbeer Ice Cream 55

Gryffindor House 57

The Slytherin House 59

The Ravenclaw House 61

The Hufflepuff House 63

The Harry Potter 65

Conclusion 67

About the Author 68

Author's Afterthoughts 70

Introduction

Hello, and welcome to the culinary world of Hogwarts! If you love Harry Potter and having fancy food, then my friend you have entered into the right place. From this moment forward, you will be learning to prepare a brilliant collection of 30 recipes that were inspired the Harry Potter series! As a child, you may have attempted many times to replicate the various spells that Harry cast while at Hogwarts and though we still won't be able to make these spells come to life, we have brought you the next best thing.

With every turn of the page, you will be able to breathe life into a popular dish that Harry and his friends at Hogwarts also may have had. Who ever said dreams don't come through?

Butterbeer

Butterbeer, in the Harry Potter books, is painted to us as a foaming mug of slightly alcoholic liquid that is not so sickly butterscotch. Now we can create a pretty close replica using this recipe.

Serves: 1

Time Needed: 10 minutes

Ingredients

- Pumpkin Ale/Beer (12 fluid ounces)
- Butterscotch Sauce (5 tbsp.)

Directions

1. Add your beer to your blender and start running the blender on medium speed.

2. Slowly add in your butterscotch sauce in a steady stream while the blender continues to blend.

3. Continue to blend until just combined.

4. Serve and enjoy!

Pumpkin Juice

It can be said that wizards used Pumpkin Juice to stay on top of their game.

Serves: 2

Time Needed: 10 min

Ingredients

- Pumpkin (1/2, seeded and cleaned, diced)
- Red Apple (1, cored and diced)
- Lemon (1, diced)
- Ginger (1 slice, peeled)

Directions

1. Add all ingredients to a juicer and extract the juices.

2. Strain the juices and discard the solid remains.

3. Serve over ice.

Golden Snitch Cake Pops

Now we can create our own Golden Snitch just like the one used in Harry's Quidditch games.

Serves: 6

Time Needed: 40 minutes

Ingredients

- Cake crumbs (1 cup)
- Cream Cheese (1/2 cup)
- White Fondant (1/2 cup, rolled)
- Golden Sprinkles (1 cup, edible)

- Yellow Candy (1/2 cup melted)
- Frosting (1 cup)
- Lollipop sticks (6)

Directions

1. In a large bowl combine your cake crumbs and cream cheese together and knead slightly to form a pliable dough.

2. Once the mixture is manageable, start forming small balls from your cake dough then insert a lollipop stick into each ball.

3. Dip each ball into your frosting, layer on a clean cookie sheet and set in the freezer to harden for about 15 minutes.

4. Next set your melted yellow candy and golden sprinkles next to each other in separate bowls.

5. Dip your frozen cake balls first into the yellow candy then immediately roll into the golden sprinkle, and finally back to the cookie sheet.

6. Once all 6 have been coated, rest the balls in the refrigerator and start working on your fondant wings.

7. Proceed to cut 12 wings from your sheet of fondant and stick them into both sides of your cake balls (2 in each).

8. Keep refrigerated until ready to serve.

Butterbeer Hot Chocolate

All this sugar is bound to make you feel as if you are flying!

Serves: 4

Time Needed: 15 min

Ingredients

Topping

- Heavy Cream (1 cup)
- Sugar (3 tbsp.)

- Vanilla (1 tsp.)
- Butterscotch sweets (10, small, to imitate butter drops on top)

Drink

- Milk (3 cups)
- Heavy Cream (1 cup)
- Butterscotch Chips (3/4 cup)
- Butterscotch Sauce (1/4 cup)
- Cocoa Powder (3 tbsp.)
- Vanilla (1 tsp)

Directions

1. Set your milk to warm in a saucepan over medium heat. Once warm add all the remaining drink ingredients and stir to combine. Remove from heat and set aside.

2. Add the first 3 topping ingredients to a stand mixer and run until the cream becomes stiff.

3. Pour your hot chocolate ¾ way up in your cauldron (or mug) and top with your whip cream mixture.

4. Finish by sprinkling with butterscotch sweets then serve.

Knickerbocker Glory

Now you can enjoy this sweet treat that Dudley had in the Sorcerer's Stone.

Serves: 1

Time Needed: 15 min

Ingredients

- Chopped Fruit (1 cup, mix and match your favorite fruits)
- Ice Cream (3 scoops, vanilla)
- Fruit Syrup (3 tbsp., peach)
- Clotted Cream (1 cup)
- Cherry (1)
- Ice Cream Wafer (1/4)
- Hazelnuts (1 tbsp. chopped)

Directions

1. In a tall milkshake glass add your chopped fruit.

2. Top your fruit with your ice cream.

3. Pour your fruit syrup over your ice cream.

4. Top with whipped cream and add in a wafer.

5. Finish with a cherry and hazelnuts.

Bertie Bott's Jelly Beans

Who doesn't love Jelly Beans? Now you can enjoy the same unique flavors Harry, and his friends did.

Serves: 6

Time Needed: 15 min

Ingredients

- Water (3/4 cup)
- Sugar (1 ¼ cups)
- Gelatin (1/4 cup, powdered)
- Flavoring Agents and Colouring (6 different flavors, be sure to include some that are not so nice)
- Oil Spray (1 can)

Direction

1. Set your water on in a sauce pan over medium heat. Top with your sugar and allow to cook undisturbed until the sugar dissolves.

2. Add in your gelatin and cook until it reaches 110 degrees C (about 20 min)

3. Spray your jelly bean molds with oil spray then set up your flavor bowls.

4. Add some of your sugar mixture to each flavor then add in your color drops and stir well so that your color and flavor mix in well.

5. Pour the mixture into your jelly bean molds and allow the beans to dry overnight.

6. Enjoy!

Unicorn Blood Cocktail

Here is a magical cocktail that any Harry Potter fan can easily appreciate.

Serves: 4

Time Needed: 30 min

Ingredients

- Raspberry Puree (1 cups)
- Shimmery Liqueur (1 cup)
- Luster Dust (4 tbsp., purple)
- Dry Ice (4 tbsp.)

Directions

1. Dust 4 martini glasses lightly with luster dust (around the walls)

2. Fill the glasses 2/3 way up with raspberry puree, then evenly add your shimmery liqueur in the 4 glasses.

3. Add one tablespoon of Dry Ice to each drink and serve immediately.

Polyjuice Potion

This sweet and spicy concoction is bound to knock you off your feet.

Serves: 3

Time Needed: 15

Ingredients

- Ginger Tea (3 tbsp., sweetened)
- Orange Juice (1 cup, no pulp)
- Peach Slices (2, crushed)
- Sprite (1/2 cup)
- Food Coloring (1 drop, blue)
- Vodka (4 tbsp.)

Directions

1. Mix all your ingredients together in a large bowl.

2. Adjust the color by adding more if desired.

3. Serve chilled.

Goblet of Fire

Will you be the champion chosen to compete for this time around? Let consult the Goblet of Fire.

Serves: 1

Time Needed: 15 min

Ingredients

- Vodka (1 oz.)
- Curacao (1 oz., blue)
- Lemonade (3 oz.)
- Rum (a splash)
- Cinnamon (a pinch)

Directions

1. Combine the first 4 ingredients together thoroughly the pour in a wine glass.

2. Carefully set your drink on fire then sprinkle with cinnamon.

3. Serve!

The Albus Dumbledore

Here is a tasty drink inspired by Headmaster Dumbledore.

Serves: 1

Time Needed: 15 min

Ingredients

- Vodka (1 shot, lemon)
- Sprite (1 cup)
- Whipped Cream (1/2 cup, coconut, stiff)
- Lemon Zest (1 tsp.)
- Ice (5 cubes)

Direction

1. Add your ice o your glass then pour in your vodka.

2. Top off with spite and finish with stiff whipped cream and lemon zest.

3. Enjoy!

Firewhiskey

This dish is not for the faint of heart as it literally feels like your mouth is on fire!

Serves: 1

Time Needed: 15 min

Ingredients

- Whiskey (1 oz.)
- Cinnamon Schnapps (1/2 oz.)
- Rum (1 tbsp.)

Directions

1. Add in your cinnamon schnapps and whisking into a shaker with ice.

2. Shake well and pour into a shot glass.

73. Top with rum and carefully set the drink on fire.

4. Serve and enjoy!

Pureblood

This drink will let you see if you are as pure as your bloodline.

Serves: 1

Time Needed: 15 min

Ingredients

- Vodka (2½ oz.)
- Sweet & Sour Mix (4 oz.)
- Raspberry Liqueur (1 oz.)
- Raspberry (4, to garnish)

Directions

1. Add your 3 first ingredients with ice in a shaker.

2. Shake well and pour into a shot glass.

3. Garnish with raspberry and serve!

The Phoenix Feather

If the basilisk of life nips you with its fangs, you will need this drink to help you fight back.

Serves: 1

Time Needed: 15 min

Ingredients

- Lillet Blanc (2 oz.)
- Campari (1.5 oz.)
- Grapefruit Juice (1 oz.)
- Club Soda (1 cup)

Directions

1. Add your first 3 ingredients with ice into a shaker.

2. Shake well and pour your juice into a tall glass.

3. Top up with club soda and serve.

Liquid Luck

Liquid Luck, also known as the Felix Felicis is said to improve your luck.

Serves: 1

Time Needed: 15 min

Ingredients

- Simple Syrup (1/4 oz.)
- Lemon Juice (1/4 oz.)
- Ginger Beer (1.5 oz.)
- Champagne (1 cup)

Directions

1. In a champagne flute mix together your lemon juice and simple syrup.

2. Add in your ginger beer then top off with champagne.

3. Serve and enjoy!

Amortentia – The Love Potion

This recipe is said to be able to help you get your love to fall for you.

Serves: 1

Time Needed: 15 min (plus time to make ice ring)

Ingredients

Ice Ring

- Red Raspberries (1 pint, fresh)
- Pomegranate Seeds (1 cup, fresh)
- Water (4 cups, boiled)
- Ice Cubes (2 trays)

Punch

- Aperol (750ml)
- Pomegranate Juice (4 cups)
- Gin (2 cups)
- Rose (1500 ml, chilled)

Directions

1. Evenly spread your seeds in the bottom of a Bundt cake pan and proceed to cover the seeds with your fruits and ice.

2. Pour your boiling water over the ice and allow to freeze overnight.

3. Combine all your juice ingredients into a large bowl and mix well.

4. Serve in a cocktail glass with your ice ring floating on top.

Witches Brew

A drink fits perfectly for a magical woman.

Serves: 1

Time Needed: 10 minutes

Ingredients

- Orange Juice (1/2 cup)
- Pomegranate Juice (1/2 cup)
- Vodka (1/4 cup)

Directions

1. In a large bowl, mix together all your ingredients and stir to combine.

2. Serve chilled and enjoy!

The Severus Snape

Here is a cocktail that pays homage to Professor Snape.

Serves: 1

Time Needed: 15 minutes

Ingredients

- Amaretto (1oz shot)
- Doctor Pepper (1 cup)
- Ice (1/4 cup)

Directions

1. Add your ice to a cocktail glass then proceed to pour in your Amaretto.

2. Top off the glass with Doctor Pepper.

3. Stir and serve.

Polyjuice Potion Jelly Shots

Delicious Harry Potter inspired Jello Shots made with Polyjuice Potion.

Serves: 18

Time Needed: 15 minutes (plus setting time)

Ingredients

- Polyjuice Potion (2 cups)
- Gelatin Powder (3 envelopes, plain)
- Vodka (1 cup, pineapple or ginger)

Directions

1. Set your Polyjuice Potion in a sauce pan over low heat and add in your gelatin powder.

2. Continue to stir until the gelatin is completely dissolved.

3. Remove from heat and stir in your vodka.

4. Refrigerate until fully set.

5. Cut into rectangles and serve!

Voldemort Cocktail

This cocktail is dark and dangerous much like its name sake Voldemort!

Serve: 1

Time Needed: 15 minutes

Ingredients

- Black Sambuca (1 cup)
- Absinthe (1/2 cup)
- Gin (1/4 cup)
- Lemon Zest (1/2 tsp)
- Lemon Bitters (1/2 tsp)
- Dry Ice (1 tbsp.)

Directions

1. Add your first 5 ingredients with ice in a shaker.

2. Shake well and pour into a cold cocktail glass.

3. Add in your dry ice and serve.

Pumkintini

This pumpkin cocktail is delicious and is bound to have you feeling like a wizard.

Serves: 2

Time Needed: 15 min

Ingredients

- Graham Crackers (2, crushed)
- Ice (12)
- White Rum (6 tbsp.)
- Pumpkin (6 tbsp., pureed)
- Maple Syrup (1½ tbsp.)
- Whiskey (1/2 tbsp.)
- Cinnamon (1 tsp.)
- Cloves (1 tsp.)
- Ginger (1 tsp., ground)
- Coconut Milk (2 tbsp.)

Directions

1. Add all your ingredients, except for graham crackers, to a shaker and shake well.

2. Wet the edges of 2 martini glasses and place the rim into your graham cracker crumbs.

3. Strain the mixture into the glass and serve.

Butterbeer Jelly Shots

Now you can turn the most popular drink from Harry Potter into jelly shots

Serves: 18

Time Needed: 15 minutes (plus setting time)

Ingredients

- Butterbeer (2 cups)
- Gelatin Powder (3 envelopes, plain)
- Vodka (1 cup, pineapple or ginger)

Directions

1. Set your Butterbeer in a sauce pan over low heat and add in your gelatin powder.

2. Continue to stir until the gelatin is completely dissolved.

3. Remove from heat and stir in your vodka.

4. Refrigerate until fully set.

5. Cut into rectangles and serve!

Chocolate Frog Jelly Shots

These chocolate frogs are to die for.

Serves: 18

Time Needed: 15 minutes (plus setting time)

Ingredients

- Water (1/2 cup)
- Gelatin Powder (2 envelopes)
- Ice Cream (3/8 cup, melted)
- Liqueur (1/2 cup, chocolate)
- Baileys (1/4 cup)
- Vodka (1/4 cup)
- Amaretto (1/8 cup)

Directions

1. Set your water in a sauce pan over low heat and add in your gelatin powder.

2. Continue to stir until the gelatin is completely dissolved.

3. Spray your mold with oil spray and wipe away the excess with a hand towel.

4. Remove from heat and stir in your ice cream, liqueurs, and vodka.

5. Pour mixture into your frog molds and refrigerate until fully set.

6. Serve and enjoy!

Confunda Chambardo

This drink is said to confuse your victims just like the Confundus Charm.

Serves: 1

Time Needed: 15 minutes

Ingredients

- Chambord (1/2oz.)
- Gin (1/2 oz.)
- Bacardi (1/8 oz.)
- Vanilla Coke (8 oz.)
- Ice (10 cubes)

Directions

1. Add all your ingredients to a tumbler.

2. Stir and serve.

Avada Tequila

This spooky potion is perfect for a quick pick me up.

Serves: 1

Time Needed: 5 minutes

Ingredients

- Tequila (1/2 oz.)
- Absinthe (1/2 oz.)
- Mountain Dew (1/2 oz.)

Directions

1. Add all your ingredients to a shot glass and serve.

Butterbeer Ice Cream

This ice cream is just as delicious as the drink. Perfect on a hot summers day.

Serves: 8

Time: 40 minutes + inactive time

Ingredients:

- 1 cup butterbeer
- 1 cup heavy cream
- 2 cups half-and-half
- 6 egg yolks
- 1 tablespoon honey
- ½ cups caster sugar, divided
- Salt (1/2 tsp.)

Directions:

1. In a saucepan whisk the butterbeer, heavy cream, half-and-half, egg yolks and half of sugar.

2. Cook over medium-high heat, whisking for 12 minutes or until slightly thickened.

3. Pour the prepared mixture into a large bowl and chill for 2 hours.

4. Pour prepared egg yolk mixture into an ice cream maker machine and process according to manufacturer directions. Serve and enjoy.

NOTE: If you do not own the ice cream making a machine, cover the ice cream mix and freeze for 4-6 hours, stirring after each hour to prevent ice crystal formation.

Gryffindor House

Here is a must have for the Gryffindor house occupants.

Serves: 1

Time Needed: 10 minutes

Ingredients

- Light Rum (1 oz.)
- Brandy (1/4 oz.)
- Lemon Juice (1/4 oz.)
- Raspberries (4)
- Raspberry Syrup (2 tsp.)

Directions

1. Add all your ingredients to a shaker.

2. Shake well and serve.

The Slytherin House

This drink will fly you straight to the Slytherin House.

Serves: 1

Time Needed: 5 min

Ingredients

- Mint Leaves (4)
- Rum (1oz.)
- Lime Slices (2)
- Sugar (3 tsp.)
- Champagne (3 oz.)

Directions

1. Add all your ingredients to a shaker.

2. Shake well and serve.

The Ravenclaw House

This recipe shows you how to create the perfect Ravenclaw welcome drink.

Serves: 1

Time Needed: 15 minutes

Ingredients

- Vodka (1 oz., blueberry)
- Tonic Water (2 oz.)
- Blueberries (14, fresh

Directions

1. Add all your ingredients to a shaker.

2. Shake well and serve.

The Hufflepuff House

Here we have the Hufflepuff house welcome drink.

Serves: 1

Time Needed: 10 minutes

Ingredients

- Pineapple Juice (1 oz.)
- Orange Juice (1 oz.)
- Rum (1 oz.)
- Ginger Ale (1 oz.)
- Schnapps (3/4 oz.)

Directions

1. Add all your ingredients to a tumbler with ice.

2. Serve and enjoy!

The Harry Potter

This delicious cocktail will have you casting spells like Harry Potter.

Serves: 1

Time Needed: 15min

Ingredients

- Vodka (1 oz.)
- Lemonade (1 cup)
- Blue Curacao (1 oz.)
- Dry Ice (1 tsp.)
- Blue Sugar (2 tbsp.)

Directions

1. Rim a cocktail glass in blue sugar.

2. Add your first 3 ingredients into a shaker with ice.

3. Shake well and pour into a cocktail glass.

4. Add dry ice and serve.

Conclusion

There you have it! 30 Delicious recipes inspired by Harry Potter! We hope you enjoyed all these potions and treats as much as we did and hope that they will all be a hit at your next Harry Potter themed party! Join us again for yet another thrilling adventure when we explore more delicious food right from your kitchen. Until next time, be sure to keep on cooking!

About the Author

Martha is a chef and a cookbook author. She has had a love of all things culinary since she was old enough to help in the kitchen, and hasn't wanted to leave the kitchen since. She was born and raised in Illinois, and grew up on a farm, where she acquired her love for fresh, delicious foods. She learned many of her culinary abilities from her mother; most importantly, the need to cook with fresh, homegrown ingredients if at all possible, and how to create an amazing recipe that everyone wants. This gave her the perfect way to share her skill with the world; writing cookbooks to spread the message that fresh, healthy food really can, and does, taste delicious. Now that she is a mother, it is more important than ever to make sure that healthy food is available to the next generation. She hopes to become a household name in cookbooks for her delicious recipes, and healthy outlook.

Martha is now living in California with her high school sweetheart, and now husband, John, as well as their infant daughter Isabel, and two dogs; Daisy and Sandy. She is a stay at home mom, who is very much looking forward to expanding their family in the next few years to give their daughter some siblings. She enjoys cooking with, and for, her family and friends, and is waiting impatiently for the day she can start cooking with her daughter.

Author's Afterthoughts

Thanks ever so much to each of my cherished readers for investing the time to read this book!

I know you could have picked from many other books but you chose this one. So a big thanks for downloading this book and reading all the way to the end.

If you enjoyed this book or received value from it, I'd like to ask you for a favor. Please take a few minutes to post an honest and heartfelt review on *Amazon.com*. Your support does make a difference and helps to benefit other people.

Thanks!

Martha Stephenson

Made in the USA
Columbia, SC
09 December 2018